FASTBACK® Sports

Game Day

DAN J. MARLOWE

GLOBE FEARON
Pearson Learning Group

FASTBACK® SPORTS BOOKS

Claire
The Comeback
Game Day
The Kid With the Left Hook
Marathon

Markers
Redmond's Shot
The Rookie
The Sure Thing
Turk

Cover Comstock Images. All photography © Pearson Education, Inc. (PEI) unless specifically noted.

Copyright © 2004 by Pearson Education, Inc., publishing as Globe Fearon®, an imprint of Pearson Learning Group, 299 Jefferson Road, Parsippany, NJ 07054. All rights reserved. No part of this book may be reproduced or transmitted in any form or by any means, electronic or mechanical, including photocopying, recording, or by any information storage and retrieval system, without permission in writing from the publisher. For information regarding permission(s), write to Rights and Permissions Department.

Globe Fearon® and Fastback® are registered trademarks of Globe Fearon, Inc.

ISBN 0-13-024601-8
Printed in the United States of America
1 2 3 4 5 6 7 8 9 10   07 06 05 04 03

1-800-321-3106
www.pearsonlearning.com

Tom Jordan awoke on Sunday morning feeling tired. He hadn't been able to fall asleep until late the night before. He got up and walked barefoot in his jockey shorts to the bathroom. He rubbed the purple bruise on his right thigh. It didn't hurt as much this morning. Most of the hard, egg-like lump was gone.

When he came out of the bathroom, his wife, Barbara, was sitting up on the edge of the bed. Her nightgown swelled out because of her near-term pregnancy. "I know you didn't sleep well," she said. "You shouldn't worry so much. You'll do all right in the game this afternoon. You always do."

"That was in college," he said. "This is the pros."

"You'll do all right," she repeated.

"I just wish I was on defense," Tom said. *And that it wasn't my first year*, he thought. "I surely do wish it was defense. I'm not a tight end. I'm a defensive end."

"If you were still on defense, you would have been first in line to be cut," Barbara reminded him. "This way you made the team, and now you're in the starting lineup, even if it did take injuries to get you there."

"There's so much to *remember*," he said. Tom was silent for a moment, recalling the playbook pages that he had turned endlessly in his mind the night before. *Slot left. Green right. M sideline on two. Drive the linebacker inside. Or slot right. Orange left. Hitch and go on one. Drive the linebacker out.*

Tom shook his head. "When I think that all I had to do before was get to the ball and throw the guy with it across a few yard lines . . ."

"You'll do all right," Barbara said again.

"Yeah, sure," he agreed. "I'm going to get dressed now and ride down to the hotel for the team breakfast."

He showered, finishing off with a cold spray that shocked the 255 pounds on his six-foot, five-inch frame. He dressed quickly in a dark suit, white shirt, and tie. The shirt was tight around his neck and chest. The Marine's exercise program for him was paying off.

"So long," he said to Barbara in the living room. No good-bye kiss on game days was their only superstition.

"Bring me the game ball," she said brightly.

He paused with his hand on the doorknob. "Baby, you've got more brass than a foundry." He smiled. "Here I am, the forty-fifth man on a 45-man squad, and you want the game ball."

"Just bring it to me," she said and smiled back.

Tom didn't say anything. He just stepped out into the hallway and closed the apartment door behind him.

The elevator took him down to the basement garage. He walked over to the old Norton motorcycle he had bought two months ago. He had done so because it was necessary that Barbara have use of the car at all times. He had done a lot of work on the Norton. He fine-tuned it until he liked the way it ran. He was proud of his Norton.

Their car was getting old, too. It was a four-year-old model he'd bought with his savings in his sophomore year in college. That was the summer he and Barbara were married.

Barbara hadn't returned to school after the birth of Susie. Tom himself was still six credit hours short of his degree. He should have done something about it this past summer. Still, it had seemed more important to get himself in shape for the pros.

He glanced at his watch as he rode up the basement ramp to the street. He was early. He had enough time to ride out to Tri-County Hospital. He purposely hadn't mentioned it to Barbara. It would upset her, and these days he didn't want Barbara to be upset.

The playbook pages entered his mind again as he rode along the quiet streets.

He was afraid of the pass patterns he had to run from the tight end position. The Marine had made them simple, but he was still afraid. He was more afraid of that than he was of not being able to block the defensive linebacker. He had studied the opposition's Number 55 all week in the game films.

Blocking was a matter of strength. Well, yes, technique, too. Strength he had, but pass catching . . . He ran his tongue over his dry lips. He had never caught a pass in college. He'd never played a down on offense. He'd played defense all the way.

He forced it out of his mind. He turned into the school grounds and rolled along the blacktopped road. There were 2500 patients plus staff inside. He parked the

Norton and entered the nursery through the dark-shadowed tunnel from the outpatient department.

"Good morning, Mr. Jordan!" a voice said cheerfully, before he even got to the front desk. "Here to see your little girl? Just go right on back to the elevator."

"Thanks," he muttered. During the slow elevator ride upward, his thoughts returned to the line of scrimmage that afternoon and Number 55, the defensive right-side linebacker. Number 55, who moved better to his left than he did to his right. Who was tricky beyond belief. Who fouled when overpowered.

He started down the narrow hallway along the shiny tiled floor. On the other side an endless line of cubicles was on display. The cubicles were glassed-in above chest height. This was so the occupants of the six to eight cribs could be seen at a glance by the passing nurses. Tom avoided looking at the children in the cribs. It saddened him to see these tiny children in the hospital.

He had been told repeatedly that the children could be helped. To a point, at least. He had watched, again and again, as nurses guided babies and small children through exercises designed to help them recover from their injuries.

Barbara hadn't been able to watch without breaking down. With Barbara pregnant again, she couldn't visit as often. Tom needed to be strong.

He walked faster toward the ward nurse's desk. "Good morning, Mr. Jordan," she greeted him. "Susie's fine and will be glad to see you."

He knew better, but he nodded. The constant atmosphere of cheer almost gagged him at times. Of course, it was necessary for the nurses to set an example for the rest of the help. And for the parents. He turned away from the desk and slipped into the third cubicle on the left. He steeled himself as always against his first look at the tiny child in the middle crib.

Hands clenched, he stared down at his daughter. He wished there was something he could do. Since Susie had fallen out of her crib and injured her spine, he and Barbara kept hoping it was just a bad dream. Susie was paralyzed, and the doctors couldn't say for sure if it was temporary or permanent. She would regain some feeling in her arms and legs, but the doctors weren't sure how much. Tom and Barbara had to face the reality that their little baby girl might never recover.

"When can she come home?" Barbara had asked.

"It's still too soon to tell."

"Why us?" he had asked Dr. Carter, though he knew it was an impossible question to answer.

"I don't know. What I do know is that you both must be strong. Susie is going to need you both to be strong."

The uncertainty was the worst part.

Tom bent down over the crib. He touched the curled little finger of his daughter's hand. There was no response. Tom desperately wanted his daughter to walk again.

He straightened up quickly and backed away from the crib, blinking his eyes. He went out into the hallway and passed the ward desk. "See you soon," he muttered without breaking stride.

"Thanks for coming, Mr. Jordan."

Tom clung to the hope that Susie would make a full recovery. Maybe she would be one of the lucky ones. Still, Tom knew that while he and Barbara hoped for the best, they had to be realistic. Dr. Carter was right. They would need to be strong.

Tom and Barbara hadn't thought too much about how things might be when their new child was born. He knew Barbara wouldn't be able to handle Susie and a newborn baby by herself. Maybe they would look into hiring a nurse to help Barbara out. That might make things easier for Barbara. But it would also cost them a lot of money.

The Wolves' dressing room shook with the sounds of players putting on their game faces. They were in varying stages of dress and undress. The assistant equipment manager was laying out necessary items in front of each locker. There were ankle bandages, elastic and metal knee supports and braces, and hip and kidney pads.

Partially-dressed players walked nervously through the small spaces. Each one was "getting himself up" for the game in his own way. "Whiskey" Bernardi, the Wolves' best halfback, prowled the room minus his uniform pants. Across the aisle, Roger Newman performed lifting exercises aimed at increasing the 50-inch chest measurement of his 280-pound body. Tom turned around on the bench at a tap on his shoulder. He found himself staring into the blue eyes of the Marine, the offensive line coach. "How you makin' it?" the Marine rumbled.

"Okay," Tom said in a very forced half-whisper. He discarded "perfect" and "great" as meaningless words to use with this smart man.

The Marine nodded. "Come in the trainer's room a minute," he said, and led the way.

The room's only other occupant was Swede Thurlow, the Wolves' quarterback. Fully uniformed, he was sprawled on his back on a training table, his helmet on his chest. Thurlow opened one eye when they entered, then closed it again.

"Number 55 is going to start right out trying to show you who's boss," the Marine said to Tom. "So Swede here will give you a little protection. On our first offensive play, you slide off Number 55 like you can't keep him out. Then run the stop-and-go. Swede will get a pass to you real quick. That'll keep Number 55 on the line of scrimmage for a while, until you can size him up."

Tom swallowed hard. A pass to him on the very first play? The palms of his hands felt damp. "I don't need that," he said.

"You never saw anything like any linebacker in this league in college," the Marine said.

"I can handle him," Tom said.

"But first you'll take the pass," the Marine insisted.

Thurlow opened one eye again. "And when I look for you, rookie, you better be there," he said. He closed the eye again.

"That's all," the Marine said.

Tom walked back to his locker. He tried

16

to blot out the rising tide of noise in the room. He tried to concentrate on the pattern he must run for the stop-and-go. Would Number 55 line up on Tom's right shoulder or his left? When the ball was snapped, would he have to go inside or outside the tough defensive man?

The Marine's sharp bark brought them all to their feet. Tom followed the horde of clattering cleats through the runway. On the field, he had no time to think about anything. The Wolves had won the toss in the pre-game coin flip. On the Lions' kickoff, "Whiskey" Bernardi cradled the spinning football a yard outside the end zone.

Bernardi started upfield with his short, choppy strides. He cut left and right, then was smothered in a cloud of jerseys at the

26-yard line. Tom found himself trotting onto the field next to Roger Newman, the big Number 77, almost before Bernardi hit the ground.

At the Swede's sharp "On two, hike!" Tom wheeled from the huddle to the line of scrimmage. He settled into his stance, glancing to his left at Roger, to make sure he had the right spacing between them. Then he looked across the line for the first time. Number 55 was glaring at him, five yards off Tom's left shoulder.

Despite being keyed up, at the snap of the ball, Tom's charge was a bit slow. He didn't want to be offside. His forward momentum was blunted by Number 55's more explosive charge. The linebacker tried to run right over Tom to get to

Swede. Tom bounced off the thrashing body. He crashed into it again to make the man take a longer route to reach Swede. Then, Tom slid off to the inside.

He ran hard for six strides and turned. Swede's arm was already descending and the ball was rocketing right at Tom's chin. He got his hands up and felt the football rebound off his stiff fingers. He watched in horror as it floated loose for an instant.

He grabbed at it again, desperately, and pulled it against his chest. He turned upfield, blasting his way past the cornerback trying to angle him to the sideline. He looked for the free safety as he saw a patch of running room, then felt himself cut down at the knees from behind.

He ran back to the huddle, with the sound of his name blaring from the public address system. "Pass caught by Jordan for a 22-yard gain." He thought briefly of Barbara listening to the radio.

The crowd was still buzzing, when Swede brought them out of the huddle again. On left formation, Tom stood in position at the other end of the line, away from Number 55. The play was a trap, and Tom blocked straight ahead on his man, while fullback Buster Moran bolted up the middle for seven yards.

"Watch it!" someone yelled, but it was too late. Fire exploded in Tom's ribs, and he went sprawling. Number 55 had trailed the play and blind sided Tom after the whistle had blown. Roger Newman helped Tom up. "Don't turn your back on that guy," he warned.

Tom struggled back into the huddle. No one looked at him or spoke. Swede called a cutback off-tackle. Tom fired across the line in a rage. Number 55 grabbed him and spun him aside. Then he slowed down Whitey Cuneo enough for the Lion's tackle to slide over and complete the play.

On third-and-five, Swede called for a down-and-out to the split end. Tom dropped off the line to block for Swede. He held off Number 55 at the cost of another elbow in the ribs, but the pass fell short. On the fourth down punt, Number 55 and the safety blitzed Tom, and he barely got a piece of each man. The punter had to hurry his kick.

"He's killing you and you're letting him do it!" the Marine snapped at Tom, on the sideline. Tom crouched down on his heels and tried to hide his rapid breathing. He removed his helmet and wiped his face. He was sweating hard after only the first series.

The Marine squatted beside him, his lean features resembling those of a hawk. "He's putting his hand right in your pocket!" he hammered at Tom. "You got a family to support or don't you, man? You're bigger than he is, so you get out there and show me something!"

Around them, the offensive line surged closer to the sideline. Tom realized that the Lions were in punt formation, after having failed to move the ball against the

Wolves' defense. Tom got up and put his helmet back on. The Marine stood next to him, his face not more than six inches from Tom's. "Get in there and show me you got some guts!" the line coach ordered.

Tom just stared back, and then followed the rest of the team onto the field. He never heard the play that Swede called in the huddle. He flew straight across the line into Number 55. He drove his helmet up into Number 55's chest, and jammed his steel-rod forearms into his belly. The man moved backward six yards, and Tom returned to the huddle with his temperature down a notch.

"Now if you'd just move him in the right direction!" Swede said. Tom didn't care. He knew that the Marine was right.

Tom was taller, heavier, and stronger than Number 55. And if he needed to be meaner, he could be that, too. On the next play he hooked Number 55's outside shoulder and hammered him inside. That let Moran cut back through the hole and roll up an 18-yard gain.

Swede moved them steadily downfield with formation right sets, in which Tom slammed into Number 55 with raw power. Then the veteran quarterback made the line-blasts pay off with a flare pass to Bernardi, who sprinted down the sideline into the end zone. Off the field, the Marine ignored Tom while taking Roger Newman aside for an earnest, low-pitched conversation.

On the next offensive series, Tom settled

down to making his mark on Number 55. Tom was handling him consistently now. Again Swede moved them down the field. But on a left sideline pass, in which Tom blocked on the other side of the line, away from Number 55, he relaxed for a moment. The cornerback on that side circled around him and brought Swede down. The Wolves had to settle for a field goal, and Tom returned to the sideline, angry at himself.

The Marine ignored his lapse. "Swede said the nearside cornerback's cheating to help out Number 55 with you," he told Tom. "When he moves in another step, Swede's gonna burn him."

When they went back out on the field, Thurlow called Tom's stop-and-go pattern. Tom slid away from Number 55 and darted into the secondary. The cornerback recovered, though, and was step for step with Tom. Swede calmly fired the ball out of bounds to prevent a possible interception.

Swede called a play to flood the cornerback's zone. Tom ran the same pattern, taking the cornerback with him. Eddie Falconeri, the Wolves' split end, cut across behind them, and picked off Swede's bullet pass. The final 45 yards to the goal line were wide open and he scored untouched.

The first half two-minute warning surprised Tom. He had settled solidly into the rhythm of the game. He was bulldozing Number 55 inside and outside, almost at will. He hadn't been aware of the passing of time. He kept moving around the dressing room during halftime to avoid stiffening up.

"Don't get cocky out there," was the only thing the Marine said to him. Tom knew it was an admission that he was doing all right.

He returned to the field, almost happy. He was only afraid that Number 55 might somehow have gotten his strength back during the intermission. The first set of downs removed that fear. Tom enjoyed himself, as the Wolves racked up another score.

At the start of the final quarter, Number 55 was suddenly gone from the line of scrimmage. Tom went to work on a younger, fresher man. It took him only two sets of downs to show the newcomer who was in charge.

Tom's pleasure in the last ten minutes of the game was spoiled only by the fact that the Wolves failed to score again. When the game was over, the Marine led Tom to a corner of the dressing room. "I wouldn't want you to get the idea you're a tight end, Jordan," he said in his rasping voice. "But you plugged a hole for us. Any man who can do that doesn't need to worry about sending his laundry out for fear he'll be gone before it gets back." And then he walked away.

Most of the players were dressed by the time Tom had showered. "Hey, Jordan!" a voice hailed him. "Want to stop off and have a bite to eat?"

"Maybe another time," Tom replied. "My wife's about to give birth, and I've got to get home."

All during pre-season practice he hadn't mentioned the baby. He didn't want anybody to think he was looking for some sympathy.

But now, being accepted felt sweet.

Everything was looking good.

The new baby would be okay.

Barbara would be okay.

And the doctors would find a way to help Susie.

He reached eagerly into his locker for his clothing.

He couldn't wait to get back to the apartment and tell Barbara about his day.